Full Disclosure

Kiera Haley

BookLeaf
Publishing

India | USA | UK

Full Disclosure

© 2021 Kiera Haley

All rights reserved.

No part of this publication may be reproduced, stored in a retrieval system, or transmitted, in any form or by any means, electronic, mechanical, photocopying, recording or otherwise, without the prior written permission of the presenters.

Kiera Haley asserts the moral right to be identified as the author of this work.

Presentation by *BookLeaf Publishing*

Web: www.bookleafpub.com

E-mail: info@bookleafpub.com

ISBN: 9789358361537

First edition 2021

For anyone who sees themselves in these pages.

1

I am not a girl.

I am a disease.

I am not a soul in a body.

I am an overburdened brain.

I am not a human to be loved.

I am an illness to be cured.

Hello, my name is depression.

-Hello

If you ask me how I am

I will say "good" every time.

But the reality is

I am less than fine.

I'd rather be facing fiction

than this depraved reality.

An imagined world of diction,

a life without mortality.

Then this depraved reality

will wholly fade in favour of

a life without mortality

where kings and paupers fall in love.

We'll wholly fade in favour of

the lands of wizards, elves and fae

where kings and paupers fall in love,

so I can read my pain away.

The lands of wizards, elves and fae,

they thrive with magic, hope and lore

so I can read my pain away

until there isn't any more.

They thrive with magic, hope and lore,

the pages grant divine reprieve

until there isn't any more.

Then life reverts from make belief.

The pages grant divine reprieve,

an imagined world of diction.

When life reverts from make belief,

I'd rather be facing fiction.

hold me here in the light

    free me far from the dark

where bubbly laughter thrives

    there sorrow sure survives

it curls around my heart

    and pierces like a dart

to brighten up my soul

    within my chest, a hole

when I've crossed that door

    when I'm worse than before

I can do anything

    I can't do anything

-Hold Me/Far Away

I've always wanted to be perfect.

The perfect

      friend

      daughter

      sister

      student

      worker

The perfect person.

But now I just want to be.

My soul is signed

with a series of scars.

They are inked with my pain,

but the pen has no name,

because names are power.

But it hurts just the same.

I can't sit in silence;

my thoughts are too loud.

So, play me a song please

to swell my head with the sound

of another's anguish.

I'll pretend mine's gone away

and I'll be a normal girl

at least for today.

I'll leave the sadness at the door

and put on a smile,

soaking in the symphonies

that distract me for a while.

Please stop asking me

if I'm okay

because I'm not okay.

I know you mean well

but it just doesn't help

when I'm always reminded

that I'm no longer fine.

I hate that you ask

because I hate that you have to.

I wish I was stronger

and could walk on my own

but I've been trying for years

and I fall every time.

My body feels battered

and my brain has gone mad.

I always want to sleep

but I never want to rise.

You think I'm lazy

but the truth is, I hate me

and I'm sick of this self.

-Low

9

My mind is confined to a cage

that invites self-censure to rage.

The words are hostile, fighting hard

but my own critique is their guard.

I am still searching for the key

to unlock what lives inside me.

Entire stories in a cell,

they crowd even deeper than hell

within the alcoves of my brain,

every phrase tied to a chain.

They writhe and claw to break away

but these bars are resolved to stay.

Sometimes the words get past the gate

onto the page, they're lined up straight

until I read the scribblings back

and cringe at everything they lack.

My thoughts are re-sent to the clink

and I stare at sheets with no ink.

-From the Mind to the Page

I've been broken

and sewn together again.

My scars sit

just below my skin.

The blood has dried

but the stiches remain.

A memory of the lost

and a hope for the

yet to be seen.

Poems are portraits of the soul,

each word reflecting a part of the (w)hole.

She floats on the surface of the sea

but her vessel is sinking.

A little more each day.

She drowns in the darkness of the sea

and her body is sinking.

This is her last day.

She swims with the current of the sea

and she is no longer sinking.

She will live day after day.

She remains in the vastness of the sea

but you will never find her sinking

because now she can walk on water.

You looked into my eyes

like you knew where I've been

and I swear I almost cried

because I've never felt so seen.

I know you've been through it too,

and masking all the signs

is nothing new to you.

I told you I was fine,

but we both knew it was a lie.

Still, you're the only one

who never asked me why

I couldn't be more fun.

I hate that we know this pain

but selfishly I'm glad I'm not alone

and I don't need to explain

how far I've been thrown

from what I thought was home.

-Thanks for Understanding

Full disclosure:

Darkness is my only friend,

I'm in a tunnel with no end

and light has left me.

I don't think I'll ever be free.

Full disclosure:

Every "I'm fine" is a lie,

every "just tired" means I want to die.

I'm only living for you,

if only you knew.

Full disclosure:

I will never tell how I really feel

because I wish it wasn't real

and I don't want you to think

that you can bring me back from the
brink.

Full disclosure:

I can still smile and laugh

like I'm whole, but I'm only half

a person, one part hollow, one part fake

both pieces about to break.

15

Sometimes I see shadows

in your eyes

and I wonder if you knew

that one day

they would overwhelm you.

We dance around the word

like it's never been heard.

But the steps never stop

and I'm about to drop.

I am struggling to stand,

I really need a hand.

The world's becoming dim,

I'm dragging every limb.

This dance of death

is taking away my breath.

-Dance with Death

17

I dance will the devil all the time,

but I'm fighting his power with every
rhyme,

because these words that I write

enable me to fight.

As my voice escapes its cell

I run from temptations of hell.

I can't change the person I've become,

the suffering I was born from.

Even though every breath is a battle

and this stream is an uphill paddle,

I can twist away from his hands

and ignore his contorted commands.

I'm taking the lead in my life,

I no longer want to waltz with strife.

I'm setting my own pace

according to God's grace.

-Dance with Life

18

The spring wind

jostles my frame

as a reminder of my frailty.

The sun shines its face

but I am not at peace.

The summer breeze

revitalizes my spirits

in reminder of my strength.

The Son shines his face

and I'm finding peace.

-The Difference of Time

I am not a disease.

I am a girl.

I am not an overburdened brain.

I am a soul in a body.

I am not an illness to be cured.

I am a human to be loved.

Hello, my name is recovery.

-Hello (Again)

20

I think I'm getting better now,

now that I'm letting the light in.

Inside and out, day by day,

I'm a little bit better.

The shadows are creeping away,

away from my eyes, my soul, my heart.

Heart-aching and soul-breaking

have led me home.

Melted, now I'm re-shaping,

shaping into the girl I want to be,

because now I know that's who I am

and I'm learning to live again.

www.ingramcontent.com/pod-product-compliance
Lightning Source LLC
LaVergne TN
LVHW010846200726
843508LV00012B/2776